MEN, GET REAL
WITH YOUR FINANCES

Be Blessed,
Be Free!   Rom 13:8

MEN, GET REAL WITH YOUR FINANCES

...IT TAKES MORE THAN MONEY TO WIN

BRADLEY VINSON

VC PUBLISHING

2013

Men, get real with your finances
...It takes more than money to win

Copyright © 2013, Bradley Vinson

All rights reserved. No part of this book may be reproduced, distributed, or transmitted in any form or by any means, or stored in a database or retrieval system, without the prior written permission of the publisher. The only exception is brief quotations in printed reviews. For information, address VC Publishing, PO Box 141701, Irving, TX 75014. 972-514-1447.

This book is written to provide accurate and authoritative information with regard to the subject matter covered. This information is given with the understanding that Bradley Vinson is not engaged in rendering legal, accounting or other professional advice. Because the details of your personal financial situation are fact dependent, you should additionally seek the services of a competent professional.

Unless otherwise noted, Scripture quotations are from The Message. Copyright © 1993, 1994, 1995, 1996, 2000, 2001, 2002. Used by permission of NavPress Publishing Group.

Scripture quotations marked (CEB) are from The Common English Bible. ©2011 Common English Bible.

ISBN: 978-0-9894976-3-3

Printed in the United States of America

First Edition

For Bonita.

*Thank you for sticking with me as
I struggled to Get Real—*

and for helping me Stay Real.

Loving You

CONTENTS

Foreward by Kevin K. Dickerson ix

How to Use This Book xiii

1. Can We Talk? 1

2. Who Are You? 11

3. What's Your Problem? 17

4. You've Been Lied To! 29

5. Where Do You Begin? 39

6. How Do You Fix It? 45

7. It Takes More Than Money 65

8. This Whole Book in 3 Pages 67

9. Why Me? 71

10. Resources 73

Are You Ready to Get R.E.A.L.? 76

FOREWARD

Money. Men will spend 40 hours plus overtime every week to get it, yet they allow it to flow through their hands like water. **Money.** Many men think that it will make them happy if they have it, yet money and money-related issues are the #1 reasons for separation, broken homes, and divorce in America. **Money.** Men often believe these leafy-green notes were supposed to be the seeds that will grow and help them and their families have a solid financial future, but instead their future is mortgaged to acquire everything they desire. And if the money is not available, many are willing to go into debt at sometimes usury interest rates to get the "big-boy toys" they want. **Money.** Men sometimes think, it will bring them peace, but money and money-related issues are the source of stress, worry, and sleepless nights.

Is this a money problem? A greed problem? A financial management problem? No, those are just the symptoms. Bradley Vinson accurately describes it here in his book, *Men, Get Real With Your Finances* as spiritual problem. The book you have in your hands clearly speaks to the spiritual issues that men must deal with to become better with money.

Bradley Vinson has done a masterful job in addressing the spiritual root causes of the money problems men face. This book offers biblical solutions, that when properly and consistently implemented will improve the quality of life of men, their

MEN, GET REAL WITH YOUR FINANCES

marriages, their families, and their future. *Men, Get Real with Your Finances* is not a quick bandage solution for problems where major surgery is necessary. This book speaks in clear, direct, and unvarnished terms about what is the problem and what must be done to fix it. This book is for men who have had enough of business as usual and want to do something now about their financial condition. This book is for men who want to see change in their lives from the inside—out. I believe this book can start a wave of spiritual change in the lives of men and have a ripple effect in the lives of those connected to them.

Bradley Vinson has invested the "sweat equity" in writing this book to impact lives of men. He doesn't merely tell you what to do; he honestly tells you where he has been and what he has personally done to improve his life. He knows the biblical principles in this book work because he has applied them to his own life. He wants you to win.

I'm proud of Bradley and his wife Bonita as I've seen them develop into a powerful ministry team and a vital part of our church. Their ministry in our church has changed the lives of many.

Men across America it's time to Get Real! *Men, Get Real With Your Finances* is more than a book, it's an interactive tool that can be used to repair and transform you into the man God always intended for you to be.

- Kevin K. Dickerson
SENIOR PASTOR, DAYSPRING FAMILY CHURCH
PRESIDING BISHOP, VISION FELLOWSHIP OF CHURCHES

*I wrote this book from my pain and triumphs.
From who I am. A husband, father, and a man of God.
My point of view may be different from yours—
but if you're a man looking to set things right
financially, relationally and spiritually in your life,
without gimmicks and a bunch of products,
using a God-honoring process—
this is the book for you!*

Be Blessed. #BeFree!

HOW TO USE THIS BOOK

Outside of the obvious, that is. This book uses new technology that will help make the most of the content provided within it. Look for QR codes (Quick Response Codes, made of black squares on a white background) throughout this book.

"Read" these codes (QR reader software is available for iPhones and Android devices) to watch videos and download additional content through my website. This is the book you can interact with and take advantage of multimedia elements.

Each QR Code you see is special and meant to enhance the reading experience. But you may be saying, "I don't have a QR reader!" No problem, you're covered too. Under each QR Code is a web address, giving you the opportunity to experience the resources with your laptop, desktop, tablet or any other web-enabled device.

MEN, GET REAL WITH YOUR FINANCES

Scan the following code to get a taste of what you'll see in the pages of this book.

> *Along the way you will also see how I handled the situation or subject I'm speaking to you about. You will find these in italics and a box, setting them apart from the rest of the content of this book. Like the text you are reading now. You can read or skip them. I added them to give you insights into my thinking while I was going through that moment in the process. I wrote this book not to come across as the man with all the answers to what ails you financially, but I wrote it to be real with you and tell the real story of how I gained financial freedom for my family and me.*

CAN WE TALK?

What this adds up to, then, is this: no more lies, no more pretense. Tell your neighbor the truth. In Christ's body we're all connected to each other, after all. When you lie to others, you end up lying to yourself. -Ephesians 4:25

I mean, really talk. Talk about what's hurting you, your family, your church, and your community. What's robbing you of leaving a proper legacy for your children's children.

What is it about your heart that makes you want money and power?

That's not a rhetorical question; and this is not your typical book on finances. You don't need to study spreadsheets, formulas or financial lingo that you need an MBA to understand. This is straight talk to the heart of your financial issues.

MEN, GET REAL WITH YOUR FINANCES

Before you read another sentence in this book you have to get your mind and spirit ready for what you're about to experience. You will be poked, prodded, agitated and possibly pushed so far out of your comfort zone that you'll get frustrated and/or angry. Expect it; embrace it, **man-up to it**.

There are practical and Biblical truths to back all points made in this book.

This is not a book by someone who hasn't had financial struggles. This is not like the books about marriage by someone that's been married five times or an investment book by a broker looking to turn you into a client.

I've been there—as a son, a single man, and a married man. I have lived what I'm going to tell you about.

I've lived in fear of not knowing how I would financially handle the next emergency. A mountain of debt stood between me and the future I wanted for my family. My marriage was hanging on by a thread. Glory to God! I conquered my mountain of debt and took control of my finances. My purpose is to help you do the same.

I am going to tell you about you—and about me too. And I'll show you how I overcame my financial struggles so you can overcome too!

CAN WE TALK?

Here is what I believe. What's at the core of your financial issues is your heart, plain and simple. Matthew 6:21 says it plain, "Where your treasure is, there your heart will be also."

Personal finance really has very little to do with money, indeed you need it to do what you need to do, but until you change your heart and behavior about finances, you won't win.

And I want you to win.

Far too long we have glazed over the heart issue we have with finances—what's really ailing us as men.

God speaks to us through His word about this issue more than any other single subject. There are more verses in the Bible about finances (over 1,300) than love, salvation or faith.

Did God in His infinite wisdom think that money was the most important thing we would ever deal with? Obviously not, but He did realize the issues we would have with it and its power to break up families and destroy relationships.

I believe God knew one of the largest barriers to getting closer to Him—and each other—would be our wallets.

MEN, GET REAL WITH YOUR FINANCES

For this book to do what it should for you, you need to be willing to do four things:

1. Pray. Brother, this book will only take you so far. Pray that you will grow in your understanding of Biblical financial principles—and how to put them into practice. Pray for peace and strength on this journey.

2. Have an open heart and mind to receive the information I will deliver. I must admit, there are very few new things in this book—we all know we should live beneath our means, spend less than we make and save—so why are we not doing it? Prayerfully, the method I chose to deliver the following tried and true concepts will help you grasp the importance of what's at stake and help you move to action.

3. Be real with yourself. I'm not with you right now as you read this book. The questions asked and the activities you'll find are only as good and useful as you are intent on doing them honestly. You know your shortcomings and gifts; you know your needs and wants. You know yourself and you need to make an honest assessment of yourself and your situation to be able to win. You KNOW where you stand right now on many of the things you will be asked. Answer honestly. Embrace the pain; correction is often uncomfortable.

CAN WE TALK?

4. Participate. Do the activities and answer the questions. You are no longer allowed to let life happen to you. It's time for you to take control!

Avoiding the issue will not fix it. Just facing it will not fix it. Working at it is no guarantee of fixing it. I know for sure doing nothing won't fix it.

Take a chance, and don't fear failing. Failing is learning how to do something right. It's time to move! Let's do something about your financial situation.

Start the participation process now.
Answer the following questions.

What is your definition of winning financially?
_____
_____
_____

Are you winning?
☐ Y ☐ N

What does "Financial Freedom" mean to you?
_____
_____
_____

MEN, GET REAL WITH YOUR FINANCES

What, if anything, is preventing you from saving money?
_____
_____
_____

How would you handle a financial emergency?
- ☐ Borrow money
- ☐ Sell something to get money
- ☐ I have the money
- ☐ I don't know

Here is what I know about this book. It will change the way you view money and relationships if you allow it to. But it can also cause the following to happen:

You get angry with me. That's OK because I've chosen to be real instead of being liked.

You get angry with yourself. When faced with your shortcomings and the instant need to defend yourself and rationalizing your situation fades, you are usually left with anger and regret in how you got to where you are. This is normal—embrace it.

You get angry about your situation. "Sick and tired" is more like it. Once you know there is a better way to live, you will realize the way you are living now does not measure up. Being angry about your situation or place in life—if viewed properly—can be the launching pad to something greater.

CAN WE TALK?

Until you go to War with what's keeping you from being what God has intended you to be you will never have Peace.

The following story has many versions. I have used it several times during my speaking engagements to prove the point of where many of us find ourselves...

As a young boy prepares for school, he hears a loud noise. He doesn't know what it is, and he has things to do—so he fixes his lunch, grabs his backpack and heads out the door. The closer he gets to his school the noise gets louder, and louder and louder. Finally, when he gets to the corner he realizes what it is—it's an old dog lying in a yard moaning and growling.

He notices an old man sitting on the porch reading the paper.

The boy asks the man, "Sir, what's wrong with your dog?" "Well," says the man, "Everyday me and my dog do the same thing—I sit here on the porch and read my paper, and he goes out and lies down in the front yard. The problem is he lies down on his tail and it hurts."

The boy says, "Well sir, why doesn't he just get up off his tail if it hurts so bad?" The man looks at the boy and says, "I guess it doesn't hurt bad enough yet!"

Why is the pain of debt a pain we choose to live with? Just working to pay our bills, struggling, looking good but broke as a joke—and dragging our families down with us.

MEN, GET REAL WITH YOUR FINANCES

Why have you settled for a mediocre existence? Where is your abundance? Where is your fight to be something better?

I want to thank you for giving me an opportunity to fulfill my purpose for writing this book—to make it hurt bad enough for you to get up off your "tail" and do something different to improve your financial situation. To help you **Get Real.**

We're going to go there. Far too long we have danced around the issues that are causing us to lose. It's time to stop dancing and start walking with authority; it's time to **GET REAL!**

"PAIN is the great teacher of mankind"
- Marie von Ebner-Eschenbach

The problem is many of us refuse to learn.

Many of us have a higher threshold for pain than we realize. We put up with a lot of stuff that brings us pain with no long lasting results. Even I have a high threshold for pain, but my threshold for nonsense is very low—I can only do "stupid" for so long before my spirit just cannot handle it anymore.

Maybe you're at that point too and just need some instruction on changing your destiny.

CAN WE TALK?

This book will aggressively shine a light on the dark places concerning your attitude about money, the things you rationalize and refuse to change. You will be called out, and more than likely be insulted—but what you'll learn will be worth it.

This book was not written to pacify you, but my goal is not to beat you down either. This is tough love, no fluff, made to strengthen you.

Let's get to it!

WHO ARE YOU?

"Who is more foolish, the child afraid of the dark or the man afraid of the light?" - M. Froehill

Money is important to me because it gives me:
- ☐ Freedom to do whatever I want to do.
- ☐ Security to know things are taken care of.
- ☐ Power to get ahead in life and business.
- ☐ Opportunity to do things for others.
- ☐ Access to things I wouldn't have without it.

My wife and I teach personal finance classes wherever people will gather to hear them—churches, libraries, offices, parking lots, we don't care. God's people and our community need this message and we're here to give it.

MEN, GET REAL WITH YOUR FINANCES

What's disturbing is that we rarely see men in our classes.

The numbers are clear, over 90% of women in relationships attend our classes alone.

Number one question from these women? "How do I get my spouse/boyfriend/etc. involved?"

Unless we teach during a Sunday morning service or I'm invited to a men's conference, we just don't see you. Why is that? I just don't get it. I must admit, my wife had to drag me out to our first financial class—but I went. Our marriage and our financial lives started to improve from that point on.

And what about women?

Men and women see money differently, duh. However trends are showing that women are starting to view certain financial topics like us, which is a bad thing in many cases.

You have to understand; women generally see money as **SECURITY**. Having money in the bank with nobody else's name on it helps women relax. Having confidence that the house note will be paid, the lights will be on and the children will have food is extremely important to women. Men care about these things too, but in a woman's DNA is woven the need for the security of her family—we tend to lean toward protection. It's their nurture gene that creates this need; many of us have not developed it.

WHO ARE YOU?

We generally see money as a **SCORE CARD**. The hunter-gatherer in us makes us chase, accumulate—and have the need to show—how much money we have. Having the appearance of winning financially is big for us.

We are natural investors, which also involves risking funds in the effort to gain more. A 2007 study by Veda Advantage revealed that men are more likely to default on payments of all types. Between 2002 and 2007 men made six out of 10 defaults.

Our buying habits also create problems. Despite the popular clichés of being forced to go to malls and carry our woman's purse as she engages in a shopping spree, we are more likely to impulse buy. To add to the financial destruction created, we also purchase higher end—thus more expensive—items.

So if we are blowing money, what is it on? Following are five of the main ways we like to get rid of our hard earned dollars. What I call "The Foolish Five"

>   1. **Electronics.** The Bureau of Labor and Statistics found that our average spending is $700 a year on audiovisual equipment alone.
>
>   2. **Alcohol.** We spend about $550 a year on liquor and beer. Pastime drinking at sporting events and bars lead the way in this category.

MEN, GET REAL WITH YOUR FINANCES

3. Cars. We love our cars. The *LA Times* reports we still buy the most expensive, fastest and gas guzzling vehicles. (Outspending women who usually purchase more cost-conscience, fuel-efficient models.)

4. Gambling. The competitive nature of this high-risk, high-return venue has our full attention. Online gambling has created a surge in this vice...playing with digital money that effects our real future.

5. Sports. Watching live games, buying tickets to sporting events and sports memorabilia are sure money grabbers for us. Splurging on season tickets and bidding on playoff tickets add to the waste in this category.

If you are in a committed relationship, I'm going to tell you something now that will pay for this book well over ten-fold and bring some peace into your relationship or marriage.

If you're struggling right now financially, the woman in your life is feeling it in a way you're not even capable of. Go to her and acknowledge it. Go to her and say:

"Baby, I know you're scared right now, but we're going to make it through this."

WHO ARE YOU?

You might want to read the rest of the book first, just in case she asks "how?" I'm just saying...

Better yet, have her read my wife's book, *Purses, Pearls & Pumps: Straight Talk About Women & Finances*, it speaks to women in a candid way about their financial situation. **What, do you think we'd let them off the hook?**

The problem is many of you will not do it because you have deep rooted problems in your financial beliefs and relationships that will not allow you to humble yourself to a new way of doing things.

Or maybe you're the man that's willing to humble himself, but don't know where to turn for answers and instruction.

The good thing is, I can help you in either case.

3
WHAT'S YOUR PROBLEM?

Personal finance is 80% behavior. How you act with or *feel* about money is your biggest issue, not money itself. Any study of lottery winners will tell you that. More money doesn't fix the problem; it just magnifies whatever is in the heart of the person with it.

I am not discounting the fact that we need money to operate in society, but simply having more money does not solve your financial issues long term.

Probably because our biggest financial issues are usually us.

MEN, GET REAL WITH YOUR FINANCES

I have found that most money problems stem from two things:

1. IGNORANCE. You just don't know any better. Prayerfully, this book is going to fix that. Part of this ignorance comes from the financial lies you live under which need to be called out and corrected. More on those later.

You are no longer allowed to use the excuse of not being taught how to handle your finances correctly for your problems. Ignorance is not bliss; ignorance is a shovel helping you dig yourself deeper into the pit you have fallen into. You cannot dig your way out—you must climb.

This book is a ladder, not a shovel.

2. A CHARACTER or SPIRITUAL shortfall.

"You have the exact amount of money your character can handle"
- Maurice Taitt

This requires you to take a look in the mirror and get real about where you stand. The best mirror I know is the word of God. These shortfalls have taken root in your life in part due to the beliefs you have about how you should handle your finances. **Stop believing the lies!**

WHAT'S YOUR PROBLEM?

The book of Proverbs calls out and describes these shortfalls to help enlighten you.

BLAMING OTHERS

You can't whitewash your sins and get by with it; you find mercy by admitting and leaving them.- Proverbs 28:13

There are some situations you are in because of things that have happened to you that you can legitimately blame on someone else. But now is the time to stop the blame and move on. You cannot have the future you want until you let go of the past. There are other causes that have placed you squarely where you are right now. *Your* decisions have a direct impact on what level you are living at.

Rather than go into a deep discussion about this, just take a look at the following drawing...it should become clear to you.

	OWNERSHIP ACCOUNTABLE RESPONSIBLE	
VICTOR		*CHOICES*
━━━━━━	━ LIFE ━	━━━━━━
VICTIM		
	BLAME EXCUSE DENY	*JUSTIFYING*

Are you living above the line?

19

MEN, GET REAL WITH YOUR FINANCES

Key Points:
- You need to forgive—even justified blame—and move on.
- You have to take responsibility for your decisions.
- Move above the line, and stay there.

UNDISCIPLINED

Refuse discipline and end up homeless; embrace correction and live an honored life. - Proverbs 13:18

Thus far you have been unwilling to listen to or follow advice that is intended to change your behavior, or advice that requires discipline. You are unwilling to use God's resources God's way—"It's my money and I can do what I choose." Unwilling to commit to giving, saving and living on a budget. You have conceded to living the debtor's lifestyle—the perceived easier route. This character shortfall has to be broken for you to win in finances and life.

Living an undisciplined life leads to issues beyond just financial. Undisciplined living has characteristics of ignorance but can prove to be more dangerous. More often than not, you know better, but you refuse to do better.

Key Points:
- No discipline feels good, but it is for your good.
- Undisciplined living is out of control living.

WHAT'S YOUR PROBLEM?

SCHEMING

Committed and persistent work pays off; get-rich-quick schemes are ripoffs. - Proverbs 28:20

If the idea was as great as it seems, why do you only see commercials for it at three o'clock in the morning? The next kit, video, pyramid, gadget, formula, etc. is the next gimmick designed to pull resources out of your pocket and put them into someone else's. Wealth gained by unethical means will never last. As Proverbs 21:6 tells us, "Those who gain treasure with lies are like a drifting fog, leading to death."

Trying to erase your financial shortfalls by opting to pay someone to clean your credit, knowing that the information on your report is valid, shows a lack of integrity and falls into this area.

Key Points:
- Looking for an easy way out of a difficult problem usually only makes it worse.
- The time you have to put into most of the "easy" ways to make quick money would be better served using slow, proven methods.

http://tinyurl.com/labpf2c

MEN, GET REAL WITH YOUR FINANCES

LAZY

Don't be too fond of sleep; you'll end up in the poorhouse. Wake up and get up; then there'll be food on the table. - Proverbs 20:13

A close relative to the schemer, the lazy look for the quick and easy fix to the problems it took years to create. With this flaw you will find yourself being taken advantage of by "services" promoted as doing things for you financially that are impossible to do for yourself. If you use credit-cleaning services, payday loan and tote-the-note establishments, and/or play the lottery, consider yourself in this group.

Key points:
- There is no easy fix for your financial problems.
- Time and effort are required to win financially.

STINGY

The world of the generous gets larger and larger; the world of the stingy gets smaller and smaller. - Proverbs 11:24

"My money, my way." Holding on to your money with an iron fist, you rationalize your behavior as being "thrifty" or a saver. **The difference between hoarding and saving is attitude.** You are at your worst in spousal interaction as it relates to finances. "My bills, her bills." "She's not good with finances, so I cannot allow her access to the account." You're not usually giving, but if you do, you analyze the recipient (church) of your giving and deem them only worthy based on your review of how your money is used.

WHAT'S YOUR PROBLEM?

Have you ever heard of The Salt Covenant?
In Biblical times, men carried pouches of salt on their belts. When a promise or contract was made, the men participating would mix the salt from their own pouch with the salt from the pouch of the other party. This reminded the men that they could not get their own salt from the other's pouch, symbolizing that they could not go back on their deal.

This is how **MEN** conducted business deals.

Marriage is the strongest covenant relationship outside of you and God.

Do you get what I'm trying to say?

Married men, if you want to win financially and relationally, do what you are supposed to do. How can you be One and not be fully committed? You are not fully committed unless you are all-in financially too.

It's simple. If you can say "our bed," you should be saying "our bank account."

Single men, be that man when it's time. Be ready to be fully engaged and committed. Not in some things, but in all things. Go in with the mindset of being One with your spouse.

MEN, GET REAL WITH YOUR FINANCES

Key points:
- "My money, my bills" won't work as a financial plan.
- You must commit to being One in all areas of marriage.
- Strong-arming the finances in your home won't work.
- Those that don't give, don't win.
- You can try to hold on to your money with an iron fist—but when God wants it, he'll get it.

> *My thoughts on Prenuptial agreements, separate accounts, etc. It's not right and you won't win in that arrangement. What these distractions are made to do is keep you from becoming One. One relationship, one life, and one bank account—it's simple!*

CHILDISH

Work your garden—you'll end up with plenty of food; play and party—you'll end up with an empty plate. - Proverbs 28:19

If you have this character shortfall you're easy to spot—you have the nicest clothes and jewelry, coolest car, the phone that comes out tomorrow, a wallet full of credit cards, and other gadgets and trinkets. Your bank account is probably empty—with no savings, life insurance or retirement plan to think of. You have equated the *look* of success as success.

You're in hot pursuit of the "Joneses", hoping to one day be one or at least thought of as one.

WHAT'S YOUR PROBLEM?

Key points:
- Unable to live beneath your means.
- You try to out earn your financial faults.
- You think "How much down, how much a month?"
- You need to realize the Joneses are broke too!
- God will only give you what He can trust you with.

You are responsible and will give an account to God for your management of His resources.

Then finally, the strongest bond to break...

HOPELESS

Unrelenting disappointment leaves you heartsick, - Proverbs 13:12a

It's hard to "count it all joy" when there is still month left after all the money is gone. When the light at the end of the tunnel feels like a train, you want to lie down and let it run you over.

Unfortunately, you have chosen to adopt this way of life as your reality. You're a "rough side of the mountain" Christian. **You believe the game is set up for the little man not to win.** It's OK, just do what you can and be comfortable—get a nice car with a reasonable note. You have to have a cell phone, so you might as well commit to a five-year contract. It's OK, get a loan against your house to start the business God "put on your heart." **This is not OK! God tells us in His word (Matthew 21:21) we can be Mountain Movers! Stop worrying about the rough side—you can overcome!**

MEN, GET REAL WITH YOUR FINANCES

Of all the shortfalls, this disturbs me the most, and is the hardest to break.

I am convinced the same God I serve that desires to free you from the bondage of sin does not want you to be in bondage to anything that can steal your hope.

http://tinyurl.com/l8fswg8

You have to believe you can send your children to college without loans. Believe you can purchase reliable cars for cash. Believe your value is not tied to a credit score.

BE ENCOURAGED! You can be victorious. There is a way to get out of this mess. All hope is not gone. Do not let the things of this world rob you of the things that only God can give—peace, joy and HOPE.

Start dreaming now! Take some time and answer the following question, "If I were debt free I could..."

_____

_____

_____

WHAT'S YOUR PROBLEM?

Key points:
- Do not adopt struggle as your reality.
- Have HOPE!
- Believe that the Creator has your best interest at heart.

Do any of these deficiencies resonate with you?
- ☐ Undisciplined
- ☐ Scheming
- ☐ Lazy
- ☐ Stingy
- ☐ Childish
- ☐ Hopeless

Why or why not?

_____
_____
_____
_____
_____
_____

YOU'VE BEEN LIED TO!

"If you always do what you've always done, you'll always get what you've always got." - Unknown

A young man takes his $500 check to the bank to get it cashed.

He walks up to the teller and says, "I want to get my check cashed." "Fine," the Teller says. "Sign the check, slide it to me and I'll cash it for you."

The young man says, "NO! Give me my money first, then I'll sign the check!"

Obviously an argument starts, becoming so loud and disturbing that the manager and security staff come out and kick the young man out of the bank.

MEN, GET REAL WITH YOUR FINANCES

Upset, the young man goes to another bank down the street.

He approaches the teller and says, "I have a check I need cashed." Teller says, "Yes sir. Just sign the back, hand it to me and I'll cash it".

"Not again!" the young man screams, "I just want you to cash my check! Give me my money *then* I'll sign the check."

Yet another argument ensues and the young man is removed from this bank in short order.

Fully frustrated, the young man approaches another bank, walks up to the teller and says, "I'd like to cash my check for $500." The teller says, "No problem sir, just sign..." Before she could complete the sentence the young man yells, "This is impossible! Just give me my money first *then* I'll sign the check!"

Instead of arguing with the young man the teller pulls out a club from behind the counter, hits him over the head with it and says "Sign the damn check!"

The young man signs the check, gets his money and leaves the bank.

YOU'VE BEEN LIED TO!

On his way home he passes the first bank and decides to go in.

Gloating, the young man says to the first teller "See! I got my check cashed!"

The Teller says, "I bet you had to sign it."
"Yes, I did." said the young man.

Teller says, "I told you so!"

The young man rubs his head and says, "Yes you did, but it was never quite explained to me that way before!"

Your habits determine how you handle money.

We all know we should live off less than we make. We know we should save for emergencies. Maybe you just haven't heard these things in a way that sticks.

To get good habits formed, you need to eliminate bad ones. Bad beliefs, teachings, and habits are what are causing bad money relations. As the chapter reminds you, **You've Been Lied To!**

Following are some of the common financial misconceptions we live under and have embraced as truth.

What the young man in the story believed as truth was way off. Many of the things you may believe about money are just as wrong but harder to detect.

MEN, GET REAL WITH YOUR FINANCES

Let's attack them one by one and see the truth.

1. Loaning money to a friend or relative is helping them. LIE

The Truth is there is a very high chance you will not be repaid and the relationship will be strained.

A 2009 *CNN Money* survey found that 43% of its readers who loaned money to family or friends were not paid back in full and 27% hadn't received any money back.

If you have been at either side of the loan, you have probably felt an uneasy sense of obligation (borrower), or some stress of not being paid back (lender). There is a reason for this, and the Bible makes it clear. *The wealthy rule over the poor; a borrower is a slave to a lender. - Proverbs 22:7 (CEB).* The standing of each party in the deal has changed. No longer Grandson and Grandparent. It's slave and Master.

2. Cosigning is a good way to help a friend or family member with bad credit. LIE

The Truth is if you co-sign on a loan be prepared to repay it.

According to the Federal Trade Commission as many as three out of four primary borrowers default on their obligations, leaving the cosigner to pay. This is why they needed a cosigner in the first place, because they are unable to pay the loan!

YOU'VE BEEN LIED TO!

What is rarely considered is why the person has a need for a loan or a co-signer in the first place. Until they take control of their finances they will always have lack. Giving someone with bad financial habits money or obligating yourself to their debts is like giving a drug addict a hit. Scripture sums it up perfectly; *One with no sense shakes hands on a deal, securing a loan for a friend. -Proverbs 17:18 (CEB)*. Cosigning is dumb!

If you have a friend or family member struggling financially and you have the money to give them, **give it to them and don't expect it back**. If you don't have it to give, you shouldn't. Make sure you are not helping someone dig themselves deeper into financial ruin by just pacifying them with money and not helping them change their behavior.

> *As a rule, if my wife and I decide the cause worthy of our money—and that's our right, it's our money—we give it to the person that needs it. Once. If they find themselves short again and need financial help from us they have to bring their budget, bills, etc. and we sit down with them and figure out what's going on. Funny thing is, we don't get asked for money twice. Unfortunately, it's not because the person has corrected their behavior, they have just moved on to others that will "help" them. We're in the business of training fishermen, not managing a free fish market.*

MEN, GET REAL WITH YOUR FINANCES

3. A large tax refund is like a bonus each year. **LIE**

The Truth is you're letting the Government borrow your money interest-free all year then pay you back at below inflation rates.

Based on current inflation rates, a 2012 tax return of $2,700 (the average for Texas, where I live) has the same buying power as $2,737.38 in 2013. This means I need $37.38 more in 2013 to buy what I did in 2012.

Let's look at it another way. That $2,700 tax refund for the previous year is really only worth about $2,663! By letting the government hold your money you've lost $38 in spending or saving power! How does that big check look now?

It's your money. Why wait for it? The goal should be to get as close to the "sweet spot" as possible on your tax return—you not owing taxes and the IRS not owing you a refund.

Change the withholding on your W-4 so that you can get more in your paycheck, rather than pay out more taxes and get a large refund next year. Look to a tax professional for help.

4. Leasing is smart because you can always drive newer cars, take advantage of dealer warranties, and not worry about maintaining an older car. **LIE**

The Truth is leasing is an expensive car rental.

YOU'VE BEEN LIED TO!

Financing a new car is bad enough, but leasing a car is far worse. You are also paying for the privilege of driving a car during its highest value-dropping years.

It's hard to even find the full disclosure of lending practices for leases because the car industry argues that leases are basically rentals and you don't need to know the effective interest rates hidden within many leases in their "fees."

Buying a reliable, one to two years old car for cash is a great option. No balloon payments, no over mileage penalties, no wear and tear fees, and no bondage.

You still may be hung up on this one, so look at the results of a study of what a car really costs to own by *Consumer Reports*.

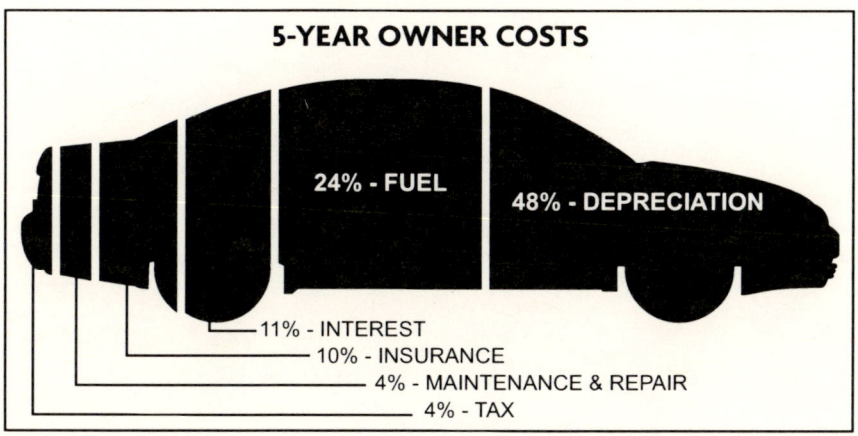

It's clear that you pay for the privilege of driving cars during their highest depreciation years. Forty-eight percent of costs in the first five years of "owning" a car come from payments, and then you give them back and start over again.

MEN, GET REAL WITH YOUR FINANCES

Break the cycle.

5. Credit Repair companies help those struggling with debt get back on their feet. LIE

The Truth is no one can legally remove accurate negative information from a credit report.

Let's look at this. You're going to pay one of these companies hundreds or thousands of dollars to "recommend" items on your credit report you should dispute—regardless of them being legitimate debts or not. Then they contact the credit reporting agencies on your behalf to dispute these "questionable" items.

Credit reporting agencies are obligated under the Fair Credit Reporting Act (FCRA) to correct or delete inaccurate, incomplete, or unverifiable information—usually within 30 days. They are not required to remove accurate information unless it is more than seven years old (or bankruptcies that are over ten years old).

Long and short of it is even if you are able to have accurate items removed, the likelihood of them showing back up on your report is very high. You are left holding the bag and this "service" is left holding your money.

Remember, it's your debt. You need to pay it instead of trying to dodge the responsibility or have it "cleaned."

YOU'VE BEEN LIED TO!

Here's a tip. Visit www.annualcreditreport.com, get your FREE yearly reports from each of the bureaus, check them for accuracy and get the corrections done yourself. Cost? Time and attention.

6. You need to build your credit score to get good loan rates, insurance premiums, etc. **LIE**

The Truth is you can live in a financially stable position without a good credit/debt score.

First, let's look at what your credit score is according to myFICO.com.

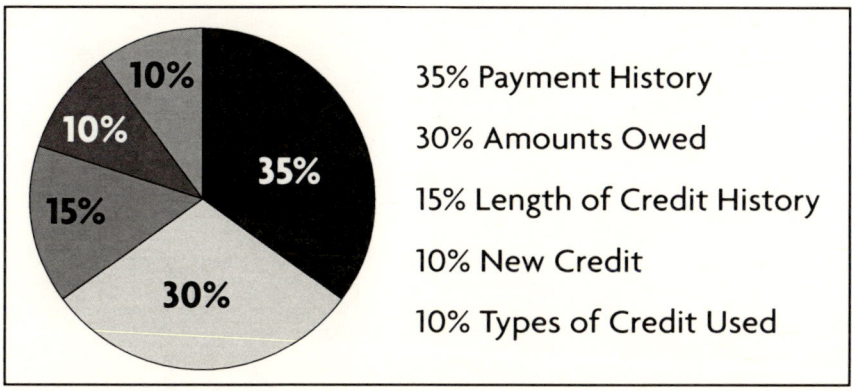

- 35% Payment History
- 30% Amounts Owed
- 15% Length of Credit History
- 10% New Credit
- 10% Types of Credit Used

Did you notice what was missing? **Income is not a factor of your credit score**. Your earning power has nothing to do with your credit score. How much you have in the bank in savings has nothing to do with your credit score.

Here's what matters to FICO—how much debt you can maintain.

MEN, GET REAL WITH YOUR FINANCES

Not too much, not too little. Paid on time and for a long time—like the rest of your life.

If you want to live on credit and function within a debtor's (slave) lifestyle, continue to work on and build your credit score.

WHERE DO YOU BEGIN?

You must change your behavior and relationship with money.

God shows you how, but you first have to determine what's important to you and what you are willing to fight for!

"We must protect this house!" is catchy marketing, but very true for you if you want to succeed financially.

You have to set a protective barrier around the things that are important to you.

Imagine you were just given a piece of land in the most dangerous area of the world. Your first priority is to build a wall around the things you want to protect. Get a blank sheet of paper and draw a large square on it. This is your protective wall.

MEN, GET REAL WITH YOUR FINANCES

Now inside that wall write down the things you want to protect—the things most important to you—the things you want, and the things you are working toward having.

Now around the outer four edges, write:
- **SHELTER/UTILITIES**
- **FOOD**
- **TRANSPORTATION**
- **CLOTHING**

These are **The Four Foundational Walls** that will protect the things important to you while you have to go out and fight this battle.

You need a cover or roof for your walls. To the side of the square write
- **RAINY DAY FUND**

Scan the QR code to download the Four Foundational Walls sheet with instructions from my website.

WHERE DO YOU BEGIN?

SHELTER/UTILITIES. In order to have solid footing, you need to have reliable shelter and your utilities in order. When the creditors come calling you have to be confident that you'll have a roof over your head. It may seem like common sense, but you can't imagine how many people are current on their credit cards but behind on their mortgage. Let them ding your credit—protect your home.

FOOD. Must have food in the house. Be careful, this is an easy area to overspend in. Going out to eat will have to take a back seat as you work this process.

TRANSPORTATION. Reliable transportation is critical. High interest, high note vehicles are not included in this definition. If you have a lease, I suggest you do your best to get out of it. You have a high car note that you are upside down on—try to unload it. **I'm talking reliable, cash (no note) cars here if at all possible.** Public transportation is a great resource too.

CLOTHING. You need clothing. Not the most stylish, best whatever. You need clothing for work and some for play. The extras have to go on the back burner for now.

RAINY DAY FUND. It's going to rain! You need cover. More information on this fund and how to build it is in the next chapter.

MEN, GET REAL WITH YOUR FINANCES

Getting to a position of empowerment with your finances is a fight. The fight is a little easier when you know you have a place to lay your head, the lights are on, you have food to eat and a way to get to work.

So now you know what behaviors you need to fix, you know why you need to fight—let's see how we fight.

Well, not so fast.

There's something I need to warn you about. As soon as you decide to do the right thing you're going to go outside and you're going to have a flat tire, the dryer is going to break, or the water heater is going to go out—"life" is going to happen to you. **How are you going to handle it?**

There's help waiting for you, but it's not the kind of help you really want or need. This help is actually a plan to invade the security of your walls. These two wall invaders are the very able enemies of your financial success.

Debt. Let's get this straight—There is no such thing as good debt. No matter how you rationalize it, debt is still placing you in a servant's position to whoever holds the "note." Even if it's used in the pursuit of more education, a home or transportation, it is still debt. Debt is bad. Debt prevents you from having financial success.

WHERE DO YOU BEGIN?

You must stay on guard. Companies use every angle to aggressively compete for your money. Just watch TV, listen to the radio or visit your own Facebook page and you'll see all the things that the successful man must have—all at a loss of your financial stability. **Debt is a product not a privilege.**

Credit. You should already know from the You've Been Lied To! chapter what credit is all about. Your credit score is not your value. Financing something is not buying it. Financing is a marketing tool designed to line the pockets of the company offering it. Chasing higher credit scores only leads to more credit, debt, and heartache.

It is your job to recognize these enemies. The problem is that they come under the cloak of services and second chances.

At this very moment you have to make a decision. Will you turn back to the ways that got you into a bad financial situation or will you change?

> *You ever been on a zip line? I have. The first thing that came to mind as I climbed the tower was not "Wow, isn't this going to be fun!" Well, I might have thought that 20 minutes earlier standing on solid ground. Here's what I know, you can't back up on a zip line. Once I left the platform I was all in. I had two choices; have fun or have fear, because backing up was not an option.*
>
> *You have to leave the platform.*

6
HOW DO YOU FIX IT?

Now begins the process to win!

There is a method and a reason for why this book is ordered the way it is. Personal finance has more to do with behavior than money. Without going through the process of discovering, acknowledging and correcting behavior the "how to" portion is just a temporary fix.

All the chastisement before, all the steps that follow, and all my prayers for you **are for you to win**. When men win their families win. When families win the Kingdom of God wins. When the Kingdom wins communities win. You get the point?

We have to get our act together, so everyone can win.

MEN, GET REAL WITH YOUR FINANCES

My goal is to arm you appropriately for the battle you face, to win financially, and I want you to win in God- honoring ways.

Along with every step I tell you to take, you will have real world examples of them working, because I did them.

If you follow the steps, I guarantee you will have success. This is not a theory—this is fact. I do not suggest anything that I have not tried (or continue to do). I'm not a complicated man. I need easy, repeatable steps that can become habit forming for me to be successful.

I know they work because they have worked for me and my family and countless other families I have taught them to.

Following are those steps.

All the insights will be told from my point of view, although my wife and children were very important in the process. I believe the unique insight that only a man can provide to other men will bless you.

Let's get started.

There's no magic bullet, potion, scheme or formulas to get you there. Behavior modification, and heart manipulation, is the only way. God's word holds all the answers we need to set things straight.

HOW DO YOU FIX IT?

Seek to be and do what God wants. **Follow His commands.**

GODLINESS

Point your kids in the right direction—when they're old they won't be lost. The poor are always ruled over by the rich, so don't borrow and put yourself under their power.- Proverbs 22:6-7
- Tithe.
- Save for Rainy Days.
- Know the status of your flock (money).
- Legacy planning for your family—Will and Insurance.

Tithing. You must do it. I'm sorry there's no fluff to explain it. You must do it to win financially. I put it first to see where your head is. If you don't grasp this and try to do the other steps you will gain some success, but you won't win. **Adopt this habit, do it**. What is a tithe? A tithe is a tenth, a dime out of every dollar of your increase. Still can't figure it out? Here's the formula:

What you earn X .10 = your tithe

Do it!

MEN, GET REAL WITH YOUR FINANCES

> *I was a weak tither when my wife and I first met. I tithed, but was inconsistent (and didn't have a local church home). When my tithing life matured, I matured. I have tithed from employment checks, unemployment checks, freelance, any increase I have had. Is my life better now only because I tithed? That is not the reason I tithe—for a better life in return for it. I tithe out of my love and obligation to Christ. My life is better because I'm working God's plan for it, and tithing plays a part.*

Save for Rainy Days. (Proverbs 27:12) You have to set aside something for the Rainy Days (emergencies) in your life. It's going to rain. You have to protect your "what" from the previous chapter. The amount of this Rainy Day fund is dependent on your life situation and income. I suggest $1,000 as a base line unless you make less than $20,000 a year, then start with $500.

You have to do this as quickly as possible. Sell something, stop eating out, pay only minimums on all your debts—**Do SOMETHING to make this happen within 30 days**—Until this is done you will not be able to move forward with lasting success.

In today's world these amounts may not hold up against many emergencies, but the reasoning behind the fund is to first break your dependence on credit to handle emergencies; second, to get you moving in a positive direction on handling your finances. This is only a starter Rainy Day fund; build it based on your life situation.

HOW DO YOU FIX IT?

> *Our family decided on saving $3,000 for our first Rainy Day fund. We had no family locally, and if there were an illness or death that required us to travel we would need to make arrangements for four people to get there, and surely we would have to travel by airplane. It took us some time to save it and not long after we did we needed almost all of it, and I'm thankful we had it.*
>
> *It was a little easier to save it the second time.*

Know the status of your flock (money). Know what you own and what (and who) you owe. Where do you stand financially? You would be amazed when asked how many men have no idea what their net worth is. How much cash do you have access to right now? How large of an emergency could you handle without borrowing money? In the Resources chapter you will find a link to download the "I Own/I Owe" form, which is designed to help you figure out your financial standing.

> *Our first attempt at debt freedom was through a financial advisor from our church. We met with him at our home. He helped us compile our paperwork and fill in a basic form. A few days later we met again and he delivered our analysis—our financial future and plan wrapped up in about 25 pages. He instructed us on how to work the plan, how much insurance we needed, what types of investments were good, and a debt payoff schedule. All facilitated by his company.*

MEN, GET REAL WITH YOUR FINANCES

> *We were on autopilot. Send in some money every month for investments, insurance, etc., and all would be well in about 13 years or so. He knew more about our financial future than we did. He knew the status of my flock and I didn't. My laziness allowed him to dictate to my family and me our financial future. When I learned better I realized it was not an advisor's responsibility, it was mine to know my 'flock'. When I took the time to know for myself, our financial situation started to change. God was so good in this area for me. Once I learned where we stood financially for myself, I couldn't stand the idea of staying there.*

Get a Will and proper life insurance. If you do what is taught in this book you will not outlive your resources. Where do they go? What happens to your family if you die before you complete this journey? You have to make sure your house is in order.

News flash: whether you want to admit it or not, you are going to die.

Get a Will. Letting the State determine who will take care of your children and who gets your stuff is not the way you want to go out. You can get an inexpensive Will from multiple legal websites. It can be as simple as filling in a few blanks and a

HOW DO YOU FIX IT?

basic Will is developed from your information. Visiting a lawyer is also an option. If you are considering trusts and other more complicated options, I strongly suggest a lawyer. Dying without a Will is rude. Having those you leave behind figure out what you wanted or who gets what is rude.

Handle your business.

> *I ignored doing a Will. Kind of felt I needed one, but was just too lazy to do it (starting to see a trend?). My wife was the driving force for me to do it.*
>
> *When my grandfather, Freddie Vinson, died I saw first hand why I had to have my business in order. This is not a horror story—the opposite actually—my Grandfather had a Will, and a Living Will. He made it simple, his wishes were in black and white—which included a do not resuscitate order.*
>
> *Your family deserves to know your wishes—in life, during the transition, and after. Love them enough to release them from the burden of guessing what you wanted. There was grief and tears, but because my Grandfather took care of his business there was peace in knowing exactly what he wanted.*

I used a lawyer for my Will, but websites like www.uslegalforms.com and www.legalzoom.com are great resources for Wills and other simple legal documents.

MEN, GET REAL WITH YOUR FINANCES

You want your family to know your wishes. You want those you leave behind not to have to deal with losing you and trying to figure out all the logistics, like where's the paperwork, etc. Consider it a love letter to them. A great resource I found for this is the *If I Should Die Before I Wake Life Celebration Planner*. A couple of pages from the book are available for download and information to purchase it is listed in the Resources chapter.

The second half of the combo is **having proper life insurance.** I use the word "proper" because although studies show many of us are insured, in my opinion we don't have enough or the correct type.

I suggest 20-year level term life insurance.

I will not waste ink or page space to give all the reasons I don't support other kinds of insurances, but I will just leave it at this…If you do what I teach you will not need insurance your "whole" life.

How much? First, let me tell you what life insurance is for then you'll better understand. **Life insurance by definition is income replacement.** It's designed to help those you leave behind function financially as if you were there. With that in mind, I suggest 20-year fixed term, 10 to 12 times your annual income.

HOW DO YOU FIX IT?

What? That much?! Yes. Just leaving enough to pay off your house or keep up with debt is not enough. Here's the math. You make $40k/year so you buy $480k of insurance. You die. Your beneficiary takes the $480k and invests it. Making 8%-10% interest on the benefit they have replaced you financially.

Many times the proper amount of insurance is not purchased because the type of insurance you are looking at is cost prohibitive, or you have been told by a salesman how much you need instead of you figuring it out for yourself.

I said I would leave other insurances alone, but I have a feeling you may be thinking of all the great reasons a salesman told you that you need whole, variable or whatever flavor-of-the-month insurances.

As of the writing of this book here are the numbers:

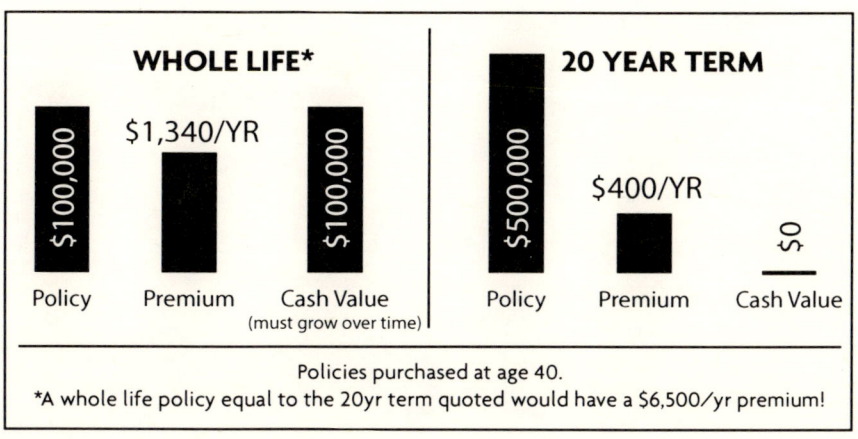

Policies purchased at age 40.
*A whole life policy equal to the 20yr term quoted would have a $6,500/yr premium!

MEN, GET REAL WITH YOUR FINANCES

It's in black and white. Once you get past the sales pitch and gimmicks, term is the most value for your money. You don't get a savings account within term insurance, only the death benefit. What's not part of the sales pitch in whole life and its close cousins is you don't get the savings account from them either—just the death benefit.

In whole life the savings account is just something you can borrow against (and pay back with penalty, i.e. interest). Whatever you still owe at death is taken out of your benefit.

Let's keep it simple. It might be OK to get your car repaired and buy your underwear from the same place, but when it comes to insurance and investments I'd prefer a professional in each industry.

Invest with an investment professional. Buy insurance, and only insurance, from an insurance professional.

I really want to hammer this home for you. Here's my logic on term life vs. whole life.

Let's say you're married, buy 20-term life insurance, buy a house and have a child.

HOW DO YOU FIX IT?

Following my plan, in 20 years:
- You will be debt free *including* your home.
- The child will be out of your house.
- You'll have a fully funded rainy day fund, and
- Have a legacy plan (insurance, investing, Will) in place.

Why would you still need life insurance?

Insurance and children. Children do not need life insurance. All the children I know—and some adult children—don't make money, they cost money. When you know the true definition of insurance, why would you have it on a child? A rider on your insurance for burial is all you need. The only reason to have life insurance on your child is if they are generating an income to help support the family.

CAUTION: Do not drop your current insurance until you are able to get term insurance secured. Bad insurance is still better than no insurance. If illness, type of job, etc. limits the insurance you are eligible for, get what you can. Remember bad insurance is better than no insurance.

> *I have 20-year term life insurance ten times my income. By the time my term is over I will be self-insured and will not have a need for it anymore. If my health holds up and I am eligible when the term is over, more than likely I will purchase another term policy—just for added security—but not because I need it. I have removed all emotion from having life insurance; it is just some-*

MEN, GET REAL WITH YOUR FINANCES

> *thing I pay for to give my family security. There is a lot of emotion tied up in insurance for a lot of families though; this is how it's sold. Don't let the emotions of it cloud your judgment on buying additional products and add-ons that are not needed.*

A quick note on Burial insurance. Preplan, do not prepay. You would be better off opening up an additional checking account or money market account and putting your money there. Last I checked—life insurance policies could be used to pay for your funeral. Don't get caught up in the emotion that comes with the sales pitch of additional add-on products.

> *Get your beneficiaries in order! If you have a family—including common-law and committed relationship—make sure they are your primary beneficiaries, not your parents. The horror stories of common-law wives not getting a dime because the man dies without having his business in order are ridiculous.*

> *A word of advice on investing. Investing is an important part of your financial plan, but don't jump into it too early. Investing is legacy planning; securing your four walls and eliminating debt should come first. Seek out an investment professional with a teacher's heart. Retiring with debt is not a good financial plan. Eliminating (consumer) debt first so all your investments can be used to sustain you instead of helping to pay off debt in your later years is the way to do it.*

HOW DO YOU FIX IT?

Teach your family and lead the way to financial empowerment. I cannot overemphasize the influence you have over your family. You are Biblically mandated to care for and lead your family. What you do sets the standard for what your family will do. Love "stuff", they'll love stuff. You save, give and spend within reason, they will too. Set the standard.

COURAGE

Honest people are relaxed and confident, bold as lions.
- Proverbs 28:1b
- You have to tell yourself—and others—"NO!"
- Live on a Zero-Based budget.
- Pay off debt using Debt Avalanche.

You may wonder why these are listed under *Courage*. From being on this journey, and working this process I can tell you there will definitely be opposition to you doing right financially—sometimes from right inside your home. This is not giving you an excuse to pass blame, I'm just making you aware. It is still *your* choices and *your* behavior that makes a difference.

The path I'm outlining is tough, and many people in your family, your running buddies, and even you may question why you're on it. Be encouraged! When your broke friends make fun of you remember; haters only hate when you're doing something that matters.

This should make you wonder why you have so many cheerleaders when you're living a lifestyle beyond your means.

MEN, GET REAL WITH YOUR FINANCES

You have to say "NO" to yourself, for a little while. If the definition of "Childish" struck a nerve with you this could be tough. If we admit it, we all have a little bit of "I owe it to myself to have [name your thing]" inside of us. You work hard and you should have some things, but you shouldn't let things have you. You have to be willing to say "no" to yourself.

Keep in mind, if you are not used to saying "no," it's going to be hard for those around you to understand why you are saying it now. It's up to you if you want to tell them why or not, but you have to explain it to those you are in close relationship with.

You have to start saying "no" to the things that are hurting you financially. If you need examples, just refer back to the *Foolish Five* in chapter two. You know what's hurting you. Start saying "no" to those things so you can say "yes" to a better financial future!

> *I remember my big "NO" moment clearly. We made the decision to move forward with this new drastic all-in plan to get control of our finances. We were looking at things that were hurting us financially, but I had a secret. I'm a big movie guy. I love them! I would spend several lunch breaks each week at the local big box store rummaging through the $5 movie bins. I figured it wasn't a big deal because I'd do a freelance design job here-and-there and I always bought my movies with "extra" money. Once I realized I was killing my family's financial plan $5 at a time, I had to stop.*

HOW DO YOU FIX IT?

> *I came home one day and told my wife, "Baby, I'm not going to buy any more movies—and before I realized what I was saying—and gadgets until we're completely debt free." It was hard, but I knew if I said it I would do it.*
>
> *This just dropped in my spirit...**Say** what you want. **Tell** someone your dreams. It will help you commit.*

Live on a Zero-Based budget. You have to get your money under control. Budgeted money has more muscle. You have to do a budget for every month before the month begins. Until you do that you'll always wonder where your money went.

I'm letting you know now—this is not easy. This is the type of budget you probably have not experienced before. **Your income minus your outgo needs to equal zero.** Every cent needs to be spent on paper before the month begins.

It will take several months to get it right.

A link to download the Zero-Based budget form with instructions is included in the Resources chapter.

If you're thinking, "I can't budget, I don't know what I'm making every month." You really need to budget. With an irregular income you can fool yourself into thinking you can just out earn your problems. You need a budget in the worst way.

MEN, GET REAL WITH YOUR FINANCES

There's an additional form for that instance—the Irregular Income budgeting form. Use the Zero-Based budget form to log and track the income you know is coming in and the Irregular Income form to handle the rest. Don't worry; instructions are included with the forms.

Pay off debt with the Debt Avalanche. This is a post we added to the Facebook page for *Your Personal Economy* the financial empowerment curriculum my wife Bonita and I developed. *"When facing a mountain of debt do you trust the people that make climbing gear (credit card/loan companies) or the mountain mover, God?"*

To conquer the mountain of debt you have, no matter what the size, you need a plan. Go in with the knowledge that lifestyle and time are part of the reasons you are where you are so changing your lifestyle and time is what it's going to take to get you out. Stay committed to the task.

A sampling of the steps:

• Commit to NO MORE DEBT! Adding new debt along the way will derail your efforts. You have to say "no" to any new debt.

• List all consumer debts (not including your home) lowest to highest. Do not consider interest rates. This method helps you see small victories along the way. Remember, simple.

HOW DO YOU FIX IT?

• Figure out what you can commit to paying extra on your debt. Your budget will help with this.

• Add the extra to the lowest debt while continuing to only pay the minimum on the rest.

• When the lowest debt is paid, roll the amount you used to pay on the lowest debt (including extra) to the next lowest debt.

• "Roll down" and repeat until all the debt is gone.

The Debt Avalanche form is available for download also. Look in the Resources chapter for details.

After you have established your budget and debt avalanche plans, remain diligent on avoiding and staying out of debt. Save up for purchases. Plan out spending as best you can. Don't let holidays and birthdays sneak up on you.

ACCOUNTABILITY

You use steel to sharpen steel, and one friend sharpens another.
- Proverbs 27:17

• Make yourself accountable to someone.
• Acknowledge it all belongs to God.

Get an accountability partner. You need someone in your life you can bounce ideas off of, someone you will allow to correct you. Married men, your wife is this partner. You can have additional, but your wife is your first.

MEN, GET REAL WITH YOUR FINANCES

If you are seeking to improve yourself you need someone in your life to be accountable to. This cannot be the person that used to help you spend money. Keep them in your life; maybe you can influence them to do better financially. *We all need someone to be accountable to.*

As Bob Sugar said in Jerry Maguire, "It's not show friends, it's show business."

Some of your friends may not be ready to answer the call on this one. **Choose wisely.**

It all belongs to God. He owns the cattle on a thousand hills (Psalm 50:10) and He owns the hills too! (Psalm 24:1). You are only a steward of the resources God allows to come into your possession. Along the way you may have lost your right relationship with your finances, mainly by thinking it's yours. **Don't confuse stewardship with ownership.**

Be faithful with what you have and God will give you more. That works for more than just money.

HOW DO YOU FIX IT?

INTEGRITY

Keep vigilant watch over your heart; that's where life starts. Don't talk out of both sides of your mouth; avoid careless banter, white lies, and gossip. Keep your eyes straight ahead; ignore all sideshow distractions. Watch your step, and the road will stretch out smooth before you. Look neither right nor left; leave evil in the dust. - Proverbs 4:23-27

- You have to be willing to sacrifice to win.

When times get hard and you are faced with difficult decisions, how you go about correcting them is just as important as correcting them.

Willing to sacrifice to win. What are you willing to do to be financially free?

Take the sacrifice test. Check the things you are willing to do and cross out the ones you are not:

- ☐ Sell car
- ☐ Turn off cable
- ☐ Reduce eating out
- ☐ Suspend vacationing
- ☐ Sell something
- ☐ Other_____
- ☐ Take extra job/overtime
- ☐ Drop extras on phone plans
- ☐ Reduce travel
- ☐ Save to make purchases
- ☐ Stop borrowing money

MEN, GET REAL WITH YOUR FINANCES

My wife and I made many sacrifices to reach the point we are in financially today. They were not easy. They were painful. Our children didn't agree with many of them. But we wanted something better and we did what needed to be done to make it happen.

I believe you can too.

Don't look at the things you may need to sacrifice for a season as punishment. Keep you eyes on the lifestyle you are seeking—a successful life of God-honoring actions—free from financial stress and bondage.

7
IT TAKES MORE THAN MONEY

Until this point in the book I have given you the tools to win with your finances. I'm telling you now that all of that does not amount to a hill of beans without a relationship with God.

It is just money.

There are many times I had to tell myself that during the fight and now maintenance period of handling my finances.

It is just money.

Had it not been for God on my side, at times working on me through my wife, other times through the words of others, I would not be able to stand and tell you with confidence that His way is the only proven way that works and always will.

MEN, GET REAL WITH YOUR FINANCES

When I focused on building up my treasure in heaven—by giving, working on my relationships and seeking His direction for my life—the money thing started to work.

I love my family deeply, and seeing them struggle through my inability to handle my finances effected me in a way I could no longer live with.

http://tinyurl.com/moj4wz9

It was through my growing relationship with God throughout the process of getting control of my finances that gave it all meaning.

Not to be able to purchase things or pay off bills, but to better manage His resources.

If you get everything this book teaches you and you miss the fact that **God is all you need**, I have failed you.

Pray and talk to God about your issues. He's there for you. Lean on Him for understanding.

8
THIS WHOLE BOOK IN 3 PAGES

What's at the heart of your financial issues is your heart, plain and simple.

Pray that you will grow in your understanding of Biblical financial principles—and how to put them into practice.

Get sick and tired about your financial situation. If all is well, stand firm—NO NEW DEBT!

Understand how the women in your life view money.

Avoid the "Foolish Five."

MEN, GET REAL WITH YOUR FINANCES

Personal finance is 80% behavior.

Most money problems stem from two things:
- Ignorance
- Spiritual or Character shortfall

No discipline feels good but it is good for you.

Time and effort are important in the process of winning.

"My money, my bills" doesn't work as a family financial plan.

Stop thinking "How much down, how much a month?"

Struggle is not your reality. Tell that mountain to move!

HAVE HOPE

You've been lied to!

Your habits determine how you handle money.

You can survive and thrive with a low credit score.

Set a protective barrier around the important things.

Watch out for the wall invaders!
- Debt
- Credit

THIS WHOLE BOOK IN 3 PAGES

Do what you can to win, so everyone can win.

Work the Process:
- Tithe and give consistently
- Save for Rainy Days
- Live on a budget
- Get out of debt!
- Get a Will and proper life insurance

You have to tell yourself—and others—"no" for a little while.

Find someone to be accountable to.

Don't confuse stewardship and ownership—
it all belongs to God.

Be willing to sacrifice to win.

It is just money.

Seek God. Pray and lean on Him for understanding.

I want you to win!

GET REAL

WHY ME?

I have told stories, given a few "proverbs," and my personal insights throughout this book. The following true story illustrates simply the "why" all this came about.

It is the story of a young couple that did the things I teach in this book.

A young couple gets married. While single, both struggled. Now married the struggle is intensified.

Both had good jobs—whatever that meant in the nineties—but still could not get ahead. Student loans, credit cards and the like had them barely making ends meet. They had over $60,000 in consumer debt not including their home.

Then they met a gentleman at their church, a financial advisor that helped them start to get on track. Working the plan he put them on they would be debt free except their mortgage in 13 years.

MEN, GET REAL WITH YOUR FINANCES

They started the plan, working diligently.

The wife heard about a class teaching the techniques I have described in this book and they went. They decided this was the way to do it and they went all in. He took three extra jobs. She stopped getting her hair and nails done every week. They sold things. They turned off their cable. They did homemade Christmas gifts. They committed to tithing. They busted their butts and made sacrifices. They decided there was NOTHING they were willing to go into debt over.

One year later they were completely debt free, including their home!

I know this couple's story so well because my wife and I are that couple. I took on three extra jobs and still worked my full-time job. My wife stopped getting her hair and nails done weekly and stopped Sunday circular shopping.

And yes, we turned off cable and lived to tell the tale.

This can be done.

Be encouraged. Be blessed. #BeFree!

10 RESOURCES

Following is a brief list of resources to help you on the journey. Scan the QR code for a more extensive listing.

Car Valuation Sites:
- Kelly Blue Book – www.kbb.com
- NADA – www.nada.com

Credit Cards, Collections and Scoring:
- The Credit Card Act – http://tinyurl.com/ykskuxz
- FICO scoring – www.myfico.com

Credit Report:
- Annual Credit Report – www.annualcreditreport.com

http://tinyurl.com/lsrdqkp

Credit Bureaus:
- Experian – www.experian.com
- Transunion – www.transunion.com
- Equifax – www.equifax.com

MEN, GET REAL WITH YOUR FINANCES

Legacy/Legal Planning:
- US Legal Forms – www.uslegalforms.com
- Zander Insurance – www.zanderins.com
- Legal Zoom – www.legalzoom.com
- If I Should Die Before I Wake Life Celebration Planner – http://tinyurl.com/mmpn65p

Movies:
- Maxed out – www.maxedoutmovie.com
- Debt Slapped – www.debtslapped.org
- In Debt We Trust – http://youtu.be/TVr813HkEjM
- ESPN 30 for 30: Broke – http://tinyurl.com/9qxbg25

Forms
Scan the QR code on the previous page to download and print the forms mentioned throughout the book.
Instructions are included with each.

If you still have questions, please contact me by visiting our website, www.ypeconomy.com.

- I own/ I owe
- Debt Avalanche
- Basic budget
- Short Term Saving
- Four Walls
- *If I Should Die Before I Wake...* sample pages
- * Bonus forms are also available

*So brothers, I've given all I can.
It's up to you to put these things into action.
I only have one question for you...*

Are you ready to Get R.E.A.L.?

RESPONSIBILITY
for your role in your financial situation.

EXTRA JOBS
and overtime.

ACCOUNTABLE
to others when making spending decisions.

LEGACY PLANNING
for those you leave behind.

• **L**ISTENING
to the best financial advisor I know—God.

Be Blessed. #BeFree!

It has been my pleasure, and at points along the way my burden, to write this book for you. Prayerfully it will give you guidance to a life of living within your purpose and God's plan for you.

If this book has been helpful to you, tell someone about it, gift your brother with a copy or several for your men's ministry or group.

Have questions, comments, a testimonial or interested in having me come talk to your group or church? Please visit www.ypeconomy.com or call 972-514-1447.

http://tinyurl.com/l38xlgr

Thank You for Supporting the Financial Empowerment Movement!

Our desire is to help build God's Kingdom with a proven, results-oriented process of becoming debt free, building wealth, giving and living victoriously.

No Products...A Process.
No Hype...Hope.
No Gimmicks...God's Way.

We are available for:
- Keynotes
- Workshops & Seminars
- Coaching & Consultation

Topics and Requested Programs:
- Faith and Finances
- Breaking the Bonds of Debt
- Whose Money is it Anyway?
- New Marriage, Old Money Habits
- *and many more!*

"I would recommend this greatly... please get the teaching. Biblically it is sound and it is of God."
- Pastor Hicks, Covenant Faith Center

"We encourage you to take advantage of this God-given resource that has been placed in the body of Christ for your benefit... so that your church can get on a sound financial footing and the members of your congregation can live debt free."
- Bishop Kevin & Pastor Sonjia Dickerson, Dayspring Family Church

Contact us to book your next event:
www.ypeconomy.com
972-514-1447
info@ypeconomy.com

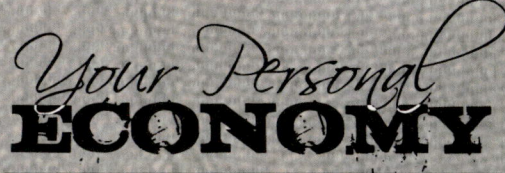

Your Personal ECONOMY
Financial Empowerment Seminars